I0136160

powerfully fragile

A One-Act Play
By Briohne Sykes

Title: Powerfully Fragile
Edition: 1st Ed.
Copyright © 2013 by Briohne Sykes
ISBN: 978-0-9875877-0-1

All Rights Reserved.

No part of this book may be reproduced in any form, by printing and photo copying or by any electronic or mechanical means, including information storage or retrieval systems, without permission in writing from the copyright owner of this book.

This book is a work of fiction and any resemblance to any persons living or dead is purely coincidental.

The author asserts her moral rights.

Please contact Sneaky Happiness Publications to discuss Performance and Photocopying Rights, or if you are interested in holding a workshop for your Cancer Support Group.
www.sneakyhappiness.com

The Author would like to give special thanks to: Claire Kidu, John Taggart, Emma Hope and Debbie Taylor.

For my friend
Vivienne Ramsey
4th July 1965 - 2nd June 2012

Breast Cancer took you from us too soon,
But it also brought us together.

Synopsis

This is the story of four women and their respective reactions to One's recent cancer diagnosis. The over-riding theme is about not letting your struggle become your identity.

Props

Chair

Gifts: slips of paper/ cards, food, gadgets, gizmos, etc

Crate, child's drawing (possibly framed or on cardboard and made to stand up), flowers in pot or vase

Table with four chairs, bottled water, cup of tea, mug of coffee, chair rugs to signify different houses

Rug with mess sewn/attached to it, lounge, lamp, side table

Old head rag, wheelbarrow with large ball, silk scarf, poster with family photos, box of chocolates, flowers, and other items representing a happy life

Tea cups/mugs, rag to wipe tables

Handbags for each of the ladies

Characters

ONE has been recently diagnosed with cancer. She has children and the love of a devoted husband. Prior to cancer, she was the glue that kept her friends and family together. Even when her friends are frustrating, she shows them the compassion that they seem to lack.

CANCEROUS MASS a dark, giant lump that is always pulsating in response to the others. If a giant, dark, Lycra bag is unavailable, it can be made by sewing two, dark sheets together on three sides with rounded corners. 1 – 2 people can play this part.

FOUR is overbearing, controlling and avoids doing anything that she deems too difficult. As a result, her husband, Laurie, is brow beaten, but her children are undisciplined. She cannot understand why the others complain about their problems while no one listens to hers. She believes her financial, emotional, and physical problems are worse than those of her friends and acquaintances, and she is always unhappy because of it.

THREE is desperate for a baby. To achieve her ends, she is constantly visiting alternative doctors and trying all the latest fads. She quit her job years ago when she and her husband, Mark, first tried to get pregnant. Now, she works from home to help support her health habits. She is always trying to fix everyone else.

TWO is a magnet for unhealthy relationships. Her husband, Garry, suppresses her. Due to all the hurts in her life, she is extraordinarily pessimistic and on the verge of a nervous breakdown.

MAN is the adoring husband of ONE. He loves his wife. He is her strength and her support. He constantly maintains his composure for her benefit.

WAITER

SCENE 1

THE STAGE IS DIVIDED INTO FOUR
QUADRANTS WITH A CANCEROUS
MASS IN THE CENTRE. IT IS A
LARGE BLACK TUMOUR, MOVING,
PULSATING.

ONE IS DOWNSTAGE RIGHT. TWO
IS UPSTAGE JUST RIGHT OF CENTRE.
THREE IS ALSO UPSTAGE BUT LEFT
OF CENTRE. FOUR IS DOWNSTAGE
LEFT.

A LOW HEARTBEAT IS HEARD IN
THE BACKGROUND AND SLOWLY
A LIGHT RISES ON ONE.

ONE   It came to me slowly, silently, sadistically....

LIGHTS COME UP AS IF IT IS
EVENING. THE HEARTBEAT STOPS.

FOUR   (TAKING A STEP TOWARD ONE) You really
didn't notice it? Don't you check yourself?
(ASIDE) I always check myself.

THREE   (TAKING A STEP TOWARD ONE) Did you go to
the doctor? Are you getting enough vitamin C?

FOUR   Did you just ignore it?

TWO   (REPRIMANDING AS SHE TAKES A STEP TOWARD
ONE) If you don't look after yourself, you will die.

THE HEARTBEAT BEGINS AGAIN AND GETS
LOUDER WHEN ONE SPEAKS AS IF TRYING TO
DROWN OUT HER VOICE.

ONE   While I was shopping, driving the kids around,
chatting on the phone, making dinner... it was
growing.

FOUR	(ANOTHER FORWARD STEP) Surely you noticed *something!*
ONE	(SLOWLY) While I was making plans, it was making plans.
THREE	(ANOTHER FORWARD STEP) I always go to the doctor! Even for a headache. I'm sure it's a tumour every time. (LAUGHS)
TWO	(TAKES ANOTHER STEP FORWARD AND SAYS HER LINE IN THE VOICE OF ARNOLD SCHWARZENEGGER AS IF SHE CAN CURE ONE) "It's not a tumour."
ONE	It's just that these things happen to other people.
FOUR	(ONE MORE STEP) My boss's wife's sister's sister in-law had it, and she was fine. She worked the whole way through treatment. You'll be fine.
TWO	(ONE MORE STEP) My cousin's neighbour's cousin had it. Oh, and she was so sick, poor lady. I hope you don't have it as bad as her though; *hers* was a bad one. (ASIDE) It'd better not be a bad one. I don't want to face losing you.
THREE	(ONE MORE STEP) My mother's Aunty Rita's best friend had it. She died. Poor Aunty Rita. Mum says she's always been sad about it ever since. Checks herself every day, goes to the doctor to get checked, even if it's just a pimple: *a pimple!* I wish that you would take better care of yourself and eat more vegetables!
	ALL THE WOMEN EXCEPT ONE FREEZE.

THE HEARTBEAT STOPS WHEN
ONE SPEAKS. ONE MOVES TO
EACH CHARACTER TRYING TO
EXPLAIN, TO BE HEARD.

ONE

I did go to the doctor! There just wasn't enough time. I could have gone sooner if I'd made time, but it was supposed to be *nothing*. So it could wait. Then more time passed, and I finally got in to see her. She was supposed to send me on my way with some antibiotics and a chuckle about how silly I am to have worried. (GIVES UP AND MOVES BACK DOWNSTAGE RIGHT) But she didn't.

BLACK-OUT.

A HARSH SPOTLIGHT COMES UP ON EACH CHARACTER WHILE THEY SAY THEIR MONOLOGUE.

FOUR

Oh my God! My friend has cancer! How could this happen to me? How am I going to cope? I've got enough on my plate. This stuff always happens to me... Why would she let this happen? Doesn't she know I already have enough to deal with! I mean, I love her and everything, but I am sure this is just going to make everything about her. I have too much going on in my life to be able to deal with this. (FOUR EXITS STAGE LEFT.)

THREE

Cancer? Is that all? It will be ok. After all, she is seeing a doctor. I am sure she caught it in plenty of time. It can't be as bad as Aunty Rita's friend, (PAUSE) surely. It's probably just an abnormal cell or something. I've got to help her... I love her so much! I know! She can do the Cancer Cleansing diet and some meditation and positive affirmations! I will help her get rid of it. That's what I will do. (THREE EXITS STAGE LEFT, WITH PURPOSE)

TWO   (DISTRAUGHT SOBBING) She's going to *die!*
             (RUNS OFF STAGE RIGHT.

                          BLACK-OUT

SCENE 2

THE STAGE IS DARK. A TIGHT
SPOT LIGHT RISES ON ONE, WHO
IS SEATED IN A CHAIR CENTRE
STAGE.

THROUGHOUT THE SCENE PEOPLE
(HER FRIENDS) ARE BRINGING HER
THINGS TO HELP HER – PHONE
NUMBERS, FOOD, GIZMOS AND
GADGETS. SHE ACCEPTS THE
GIFTS NUMBLY, BUT IGNORES
WHO IS BRINGING IT.

ONE   My breath has been knocked from me

Nothing but dark surrounds me

The walls are closing in on me

Surely this truth it cannot be

People are coming to help me

Fixing and enveloping me

With sad faces full of sympathy

And instructions to think positively

Their love is crowding in on me

All I want to do is flee...

Flee...

Flee.

LIGHT FADES OR CLOSES A LITTLE
WITH EACH "FLEE," AND THE LAST
ONE CREATES A BLACK OUT.

SCENE 3

THE CANCEROUS MASS SITS, CROSS-LEGGED IN THE MIDDLE OF THE ROOM. ONE IS LEANING UP AGAINST IT, AS THOUGH IT IS HER HOSPITAL BED.

A CHILD'S DRAWING SHOULD BE NEXT TO THE BED ON A SMALL CRATE THAT SERVES AS A SIDE TABLE.

THE LIGHTING IS STARK AND BRIGHT LIKE THE ARTIFICIAL LIGHTS OF A HOSPITAL. IN THE BACKGROUND, WE HEAR MEDICAL EQUIPMENT.

THREE WALKS ONSTAGE FROM STAGE RIGHT AND HANDS FLOWERS TO ONE. SHE DOESN'T MAKE EYE CONTACT WITH ONE OR WITH THE CANCEROUS MASS DURING THE ENTIRE MONOLOGUE.

THREE   (UNCOMFORTABLE AND SAD) Surgery went well, then?

Oh, I meant to tell you. We got the tests back from our latest IVF. (PAUSE) It didn't work. Mark says he's done. That was our seventh round. It's just too expensive. Mark says we have no equity left to use, and I need to be happy with our puppies. And I am. I think we weren't meant to have kids (NERVOUS LAUGH)

Really, I'm just worried about him. He bought a Bronco's baby suit during round one of the treatments.

ONE REACHES OUT AND GRABS

THREE'S HAND.

He doesn't know that I know, but I do, and... Oh, you don't need to hear this! I'll see you later.

THREE PULLS HER HAND AWAY AND EXITS STAGE RIGHT.

TWO ENTERS STAGE RIGHT IN A RUSH.

TWO   Hi, ya! I just ducked in between errands. I had to drop off Garry's dry cleaning and pick up something for our dinner, so I was in the neighbourhood. How are you?

TWO TOUCHES THE CANCEROUS MASS ON THE HEAD AS IF STROKING ONE'S HAIR.

(DISTRACTEDLY) Have they said.... how much time you've got?

TWO REALIZES WHAT SHE IS DOING AND PULLS AWAY QUICKLY.

I'd love to spend more time with you, but if Garry gets home and I haven't finished the vacuuming, he will lose it! Men!

How's yours coping at home with you gone so much and with all the kids to look after? My Garry says if it were us, he would take a cruise to the islands to help reduce his stress and get my Mum to come and look after April. (TITTERS NERVOUSLY THEN STOPS ABRUPTLY) He would too, you know.

Do you remember when she was born? He went to that log cabin for a couple of weeks. You know, he is always thinking of me, and he wanted to give me space and time to adjust to my new role. But I got him back! I hired a cleaner to help me while he was gone! He has never found out to this day! Of course, I had to borrow the money for the cleaner off my Mum because Garry does our finances you know.

Capable of taking care of all his money, he says. What's mine is mine, and what's yours is mine. (TITTERS NERVOUSLY AGAIN) He is such a crack up!

> ONE REACHES OUT AND GRABS TWO'S HAND.

> TWO IS STILL LAUGHING DISTRACTEDLY, BUT HER VOICE FALLS OFF BECAUSE EVEN SHE DOES NOT THINK HER LIFE IS FUNNY.

Anyway I have to go.

> TWO GIVES A WEAK SMILE, PULLS HER HAND AWAY AND SALUTES.

Don't want to make the boss angry!

> TWO EXITS STAGE RIGHT.

> ONE CLOSES HER EYES AND DOZES THE LIGHTS SHIFT TO A SOFT, PINK WASH.

CHILD   (OFFSTAGE) *Mummy, don't leave me! I still need you...*

> ONE WAKES WITH A START. SHE REACHES OVER TO THE PICTURE AND LOOKS AT IT.

> WE HEAR THE LOW HEARTBEAT

OVER THE MEDICAL EQUIPMENT.
THE LIGHTS COME UP ABRUPTLY
AND ONE PLACES THE PICTURE
BACK.

FOUR WALKS IN FROM STAGE
RIGHT, FLUSTERED. HER EYES FALL
ON THE FLOWERS.

FOUR   (JEALOUSLY) Flowers, hey? You lucky girl! I
never get flowers. Laurie hasn't a romantic
bone in his body.

(EMBARRASSED THAT SHE IS THE LAST TO
COME) I've wanted to come to see you, but I've
just been so down. I haven't been able to get
out the door. Oh, and I've had a really aching
toe. It's even been keeping me up at night. I've
gotten absolutely no sleep! And do you think
Laurie cares? Of course not.

I hate that... not sleeping. I get so... so tired ...
and then there's my toe. Throbbing all night.

FOUR WANDERS OVER TO THE
SIDE TABLE AND EXAMINES THE
PICTURE AND FLOWERS.

Then, you know, once I'm awake, I think about
work. My boss is such an arsehole. He always
gets angry with me for no reason. Ugh, work!
Can you believe they didn't approve my leave?
I was so angry. Then I had to get into my shitty
car and drive home with the windows down
cause the air con's broken. Broken! In the
middle of the summer! Can you believe it? So,
I've spent the last few days at home, feeling
low. I have been so down, and nobody
understands.

FOUR WANDERS OVER TO WHERE
A TELEVISION WOULD BE AND

PRETENDS TO TURN IT ON.

I called in sick yesterday. That'll teach them. Just been sitting around watching Dr Phil. (SIGHS) I wish I had a bigger TV. My neighbour just got a new one. One of those 3D fancy things. Can you believe it!? Bitch. She gets everything. Oh, and they simply "must get a new Prado!" "Theirs is 3 years old now!" *Gag!!* How sad for them!

FOUR WALKS BACK TO THE BED-SIDE AND TRIES TO MAKE THE CANCEROUS MASS UNDERSTAND HER POSITION.

Know what I mean? I'm not trying to complain. I'm just sick of my life being so unfair! I feel as if there is a person standing behind me with an axe just waiting to hook into me with another setback. Or, perhaps it's more as if I am an ant, and a giant boot is trying to squash me into the ground! Anyway, I need a rest. Being at hospitals really drains me. I suppose you will probably need me to come back and cheer you up again tomorrow, so I will do my best to fit it in.

ONE RELEASES FOUR'S HAND.

FOUR TURNS AND EXITS STAGE RIGHT. HALFWAY THERE, SHE BEGINS TO LIMP WITH HER SORE TOE.

BLACK-OUT

SCENE 4

> TWO, THREE AND FOUR ARE IN A COFFEE SHOP, SITTING AROUND A TABLE IN THE MIDDLE OF THE AFTERNOON WITH AN EMPTY CHAIR WHERE ONE WOULD HAVE SAT.
>
> THE WAIT STAFF BRINGS TWO A BOTTLED WATER, THREE HERBAL TEA, AND FOUR A MUG OF COFFEE.

THREE   (TO WAITER) Organic?

> THE WAITER NODS SAGELY.

I still can't believe this is happening to us. I was talking to Mum, and she said that Aunty Rita said she should be collecting cobbler's pegs. You know: those little weeds with the annoying black bits that get stuck to your clothes. Aunty Rita said that she needs to collect the whole plant and to boil it into a tea. If she drinks a tablespoon every hour, it will cure her cancer. Aunty Rita said that if her friend had done that then she wouldn't have died.

TWO   I hope she doesn't die...What will I do if she dies?

FOUR   (IGNORING TWO) That's not what I heard. I've heard you have to drink your first morning's wee.

TWO & THREE   (TOGETHER) Eww, that's gross!

FOUR   Don't you think it is worth asking her to make this small sacrifice, in order to get her better?

TWO   (ALARMED) Of course! We don't want her to die!

FOUR   Precisely. I know for a fact that the American Indians used it, and we all know how healthy they are.

> TWO IS CONFUSED. THREE ROLLS
> HER EYES.

(TO THREE) You should make her! She listens to you.

THREE   (STARTLED) I'm not telling her to drink her own urine! That's ridiculous! I have never heard of such a crazy cure.

I *am* going to talk to her about eating better. I've seen her eating so much crap. I didn't want to say anything, (WHISPERED) but don't you think that's why she got cancer?

> FOUR ROLLS HER EYES AND TAPS
> HER FOOT IMPATIENTLY.

I've read so many books about trying to conceive, and they all emphasise the importance of a balanced diet. It seems to me that if a woman must eat right to have a baby, she should also eat right to avoid getting cancer.

> TWO NODS IN AGREEMENT WITH
> THREE AND GLANCES NERVOUSLY
> AT FOUR.

FOUR   (TALKING OVER THREE) Ugh. All you can think about is having a baby. Do you want us to buy you a T-shirt that says, "I want a baby"? (PAUSE) Parenthood is not all it's cracked up to be you know!

> THREE GLARES AT FOUR FOR A
> MOMENT AND THEN DISMISSES
> HER COMMENT.

THREE   Anyway, as I was saying... She hasn't really had a good diet for some time: all those soft drinks and that cheesy pasta. I wouldn't usually say anything but.... well... now she has cancer. It's only to be expected. I have tried to get her to join me at Zumba or Hot Yoga, too, but she never seems that interested.

> TWO NODS TO SHOW HER SUPPORT OF THREE.
>
> FOUR DECIDES HER SORE TOE IS MORE INTERESTING THAN THE CONVERSATION AND BEGINS EXAMINING IT.

I have learned over the years to be really careful with what I eat and to make sure that I exercise regularly. *All* the baby books say that Mark's and my health is so important. Because, (SHEEPISHLY) well you know, we have wanted a baby for so long. I need to keep my body baby ready.

TWO   (WARMLY) I love how focused you are. Of course when it comes to food, I just have to cook what Garry tells me. He wouldn't eat just any old thing! And he would hit the roof if I started asking for money for something like Hot Yoga! (GIGGLE)

THREE   I know! I just wish I could get the health message out there! I think it would make such a difference in people's lives.

FOUR   Well, I highly doubt she got cancer because of the food she eats. For goodness' sake, even babies get cancer... did they eat something wrong to get it?

THREE   Of course not! (ASIDE) Though, I wouldn't know anything about babies would I?

TWO   Is it bad to say that I'm glad that it's not me

who got breast cancer? Garry's a boob man. He says he wouldn't stick around if I became half a woman.

THREE   (INCREDULOUS) She's not half a woman!

FOUR   (DEFENSIVELY) That's a terrible thing to say about my friend... My friend is a complete woman, thank you very much... I wouldn't have her in my life otherwise.

TWO   Sorry, it's not me that thinks that! (LOOKS AT THREE THEN FOUR) You know I wouldn't say that about her! I was just talking to Garry about it, and well, he said... (TWO RETHINKS HER WORDS) Forget about it. I just don't want her to die.... I'm so worried she's going to die. (GLANCING AT THE EMPTY CHAIR IN HORROR)

THREE   (UPSET) She's not going to die!

FOUR   (TALKING TO HERSELF) She'd better not. How would I cope? I would be so upset people probably wouldn't know how to console me at the funeral. (AFFIRMATIVELY) She won't die.

THREE   (ASIDE) She'd better not die! She's the only one who really understands how sad I am about not having a baby.

TWO   (WORRIED) What if she dies? What if I die?

FOUR   She won't die. Breast cancer is the best kind of cancer to get. It's like the "good cancer."

THREE   "Good cancer?" How can any cancer be good?

FOUR   I mean, you're lucky, right? You don't *need* a boob! It's not an important part of you.

TWO   It's pretty important to Garry!

THREE   But Garry's an idiot. I mean, having a breast is not important compared with living... but it's still important. I just couldn't go through what she's going through. That's why I take such good care of my body. Well that, and to make sure--

FOUR   (INTERRUPTING AND ROLLING EYES) --that it's always baby ready.

BLACK-OUT

SCENE 5

THE STAGE IS BLACK WITH A SPOT
ON ONE AND CANCEROUS MASS.

ONE IS SITTING CROSS-LEGGED
IN FRONT OF THE CANCEROUS
MASS THINKING ABOUT HER
FRIENDS.

ONE

I'm sorry to inconvenience you.
I'll try to do my best
To wear a brave face, slap on a smile
And not require too much rest.

I'm sorry if I appear selfish
With my requests, fatigue and complaints.
I really wish to not to be this way
But clearly that wishing's in vain.

I'm sorry I've become a burden:
That I no longer give, but I take.
I'm hoping your vision comes to fruition,
And I am fine, no needs to make.

But what if this battle gets worse yet?
What if this road's only the start?
If self-sufficiency is a thing of the past,
And I need more nurture of my heart?

I'm sorry this thing isn't easy.
I'd throw it away if I could.
But knowing it's me and not any of you,
Makes me glad, as it should.

THE LIGHTS RISE AND ONE
STANDS AND TURNS TO VENT
HER ANGER ON THE CANCEROUS
MASS. SHE BEGINS TO TRY TO
MOVE IT OUT OF HER LIFE. AT
TIMES, SHE IS PUSHING THE CANCER.
AT OTHER TIMES, IT IS PULLING
HER.

I'll get through this,

> PAUSE – STRUGGLE. ONE APPEARS
> TO WIN.

(CONVICTED) I'm so strong,

> PAUSE – STRUGGLE. CANCEROUS
> MASS APPEARS TO WIN.

(SARCASTIC) Cool, calm and collected.

> PAUSE – STRUGGLE. ONE APPEARS
> TO WIN.

(DECISIVE) There's nothing wrong!

> PAUSE – STRUGGLE. ONE APPEARS
> TO WIN.

(BUILDING) Nothing's going to stop me now!

> PAUSE – STRUGGLE. CANCEROUS
> MASS APPEARS TO WIN.

(DETERMINED) I'm *coming* through this

> PAUSE – STRUGGLE. ONE APPEARS
> TO WIN.

(MORE DETERMINED) not *going* through this!

> PAUSE – STRUGGLE. CANCEROUS
> MASS APPEARS TO WIN.

(UNSURE) If it doesn't kill me, it'll make me stronger?

> PAUSE – STRUGGLE. CANCEROUS
> MASS APPEARS TO WIN.

(SARCASTIC) Stay positive. That's the key.

> PAUSE – STRUGGLE. ONE APPEARS
> TO WIN.

(UNSURE) Hundreds of women go through this
every day,

> PAUSE – STRUGGLE. ONE APPEARS
> TO WIN.

...and everyone keeps telling me how well they
all seem to do it...

> PAUSE – STRUGGLE. CANCEROUS
> MASS APPEARS TO WIN.

(QUESTIONING) I am just the strong and silent
type.

> PAUSE – STRUGGLE. ONE APPEARS
> TO WIN.

(MEDITATIVELY) My body is a temple.

> PAUSE – STRUGGLE. CANCEROUS
> MASS APPEARS TO WIN.

(SCREAMING AND GIVING CANCEROUS MASS A
BIG SHOVE) Just get out of me! I didn't invite
you to be here!

> LIGHTS FADE OUT WITH NO
> RESOLUTION AS TO WHOM WON
> THE BATTLE. IDEALLY, BOTH WILL
> END UP IN THE SAME POSITION
> THEY BEGAN IN WITH ONE SITTING
> CROSS-LEGGED IN FRONT OF THE
> CANCEROUS MASS TO REST.

SCENE 6

LIGHTS COME UP ON FOUR'S
HOME. HER HOME SHOULD
REFLECT COMFORT, BUT EVERY-
THING SHOULD BE WELL WORN
AND PERHAPS A LITTLE
MISMATCHED. WE SEE A MESS
SCATTERED ON THE RUG, A
LOUNGE, AND A LAMP ON A SIDE
TABLE.

FOUR, THREE AND TWO ENTER
TOGETHER AND SIT.

FOUR   I'm so glad you finally could come to my
            house. Excuse the mess. Laurie does nothing
            to help around here, you know.

TWO   Oh! Do you want me to start cleaning up or
            something?

FOUR   No! No. Let's just enjoy our tea. You can give
            me a hand later.

            AWKWARD SILENCE. THEY GLANCE
            AT THE EMPTY CHAIR.

            Well, what have you girls been up to anyway?

THREE   (PROUDLY) I've taken up writing!

FOUR   What? What about Pottery? Weren't you doing
            pottery?

THREE   (SHRUGS) Well, I used to do pottery, but now
            I'm doing writing. It's so fantastic!

TWO   That's great! I would love to take a class one
            day...

THREE   Well, why don't you?

TWO   (NERVOUSLY) I don't think that Garry would ap prove.

FOUR   Are you kidding me? In my household, it's Laurie who has to ask *me* permission!

TWO LOOKS AS IF IT HAS NEVER OCCURRED TO HER TO TELL HER HUSBAND WHAT TO DO. THREE PATS TWO'S LEG UNDERSTAND-INGLY.

THREE   I think you should do what makes you happy. You know, you only get one chance at life...

THERE IS ANOTHER BRIEF PAUSE.

THREE UNCONSCIOUSLY HOLDS HER BELLY, TWO LOOKS DISTRESSED AS IF SHE DOESN'T KNOW WHAT SHE WANTS IN HER LIFE, AND FOUR LOOKS AT THE MESS OF HER HOUSE, WISHING SHE COULD AFFORD TO PAY SOMEONE TO CLEAN IT.

THREE   ...and some of us don't even get that.

FOUR   Doing a class of some sort *would* make me happy. But not everyone can just go and sign up for any old class they want. Laurie doesn't make enough for me to flit about like some people.

ANOTHER UNCOMFORTABLE SILENCE FILLS THE AIR. AGAIN THE WOMEN LOOK TO THE EMPTY CHAIR.

FOUR   Well, go on then. Tell us all about your latest thing.

THREE	(EMBARRASSED AND TIMID) Um... yeah... sure. I just started taking a children's picture book writing class.
FOUR	(ASTONISHED) What? Picture books for children?
TWO	(WORRIED) Oh! Are you *sure* you should be writing books for children?
THREE	(FIRMLY, AS IF REHEARSED) Yes, I'm writing a book for children. (SHEEPISHLY) Actually, it was Mark's idea. He thought it would be good for me.
FOUR	*Hello!* You don't have any children!
	UNCOMFORTABLE SILENCE. FOUR AND THREE LOCK EYES.
TWO	(BLURTS OUT TO FOUR IN AN EFFORT TO SAVE THE CONVERSATION) Um, can I get you a drink or something?
FOUR	(SCOWLS) No, this is my house! I can get my own drink if I want it!
TWO	(MEEKLY) Sorry.
THREE	I wish she could be here. (GLARES AT FOUR) She always knows the right thing to say.
FOUR	Have both of you gone batty? One minute we are talking about writing books for children, of all things, because you (POINTING AT THREE) have decided that's a good idea. Then, you (POINTS AT TWO) offer me something to drink in my own home! Now, apparently you're wishing that I invited someone here to make better conversation, when all I've done is let you talk about what you want!
THREE	You know what I mean. I miss her; that's all. I

think it's so sad that she's sick. She understands me.

FOUR   Oh, and I guess by that you mean that I don't understand you? I'll tell you what I do understand: children. *I* could write a children's book or two. I know exactly what children like. I think you can tell that by just looking at my children. They are *such* darlings--

> THREE MOUTHS 'DARLINGS' TO TWO, AND TWO RESTRAINS A GIGGLE.

--(FOUR CONTINUES WITHOUT SEEING THEM) And I don't want her to be sick either, but there are lots of us out here who have problems. (FOUR GESTURES TO HERSELF)

> FOUR, THREE AND TWO FREEZE FACING WISTFULLY INTO THE AUDIENCE.

> LIGHTS DIM TO BLACK LEAVING A SPOT ON EACH OF THE WOMEN.

THREE   (ASIDE) I wish I could stop wanting a baby.

TWO   (ASIDE) I wish I could make everyone happy.

FOUR   (ASIDE) I wish they could understand how it feels to be me.

BLACK-OUT

SCENE 7

ONE SITS DEJECTEDLY IN A CHAIR CENTRE STAGE LEFT WEARING A SCARF TO COVER HER HEAD AND LOOKING LONGINGLY AT A WHEELBARROW CENTRE STAGE RIGHT.

THE CANCEROUS MASS IS DIRECTLY CENTRE STAGE OBSCURING ONE'S VIEW. FLOWERS, A LARGE BALL, A STIFF POSTER BOARD WITH PICTURES GLUED TO IT AND A LARGE BOX OF CHOCOLATES SIT VISIBLY PEEKING OUT FROM THE WHEELBARROW, AND A SILK SCARF.

MAN STANDS BESIDE THE WHEEL-BARROW AND SPEAKS TO ONE. HOWEVER, ONCE ONE SPEAKS SHE ONLY LOOKS AT AND SPEAKS TO THE AUDIENCE.

THE LIGHTING IS SOMBRE WITH A WIDE SPOTLIGHT ON THE WHEEL-BARROW/MAN MARKING THE BRIGHTEST POINT ON THE STAGE AND THE AREA AROUND ONE BEING THE GLOOMIEST AREA.

ONE   (TO AUDIENCE) I have realised since my cancer diagnosis not to worry when other people moan about what is going on for them because it is exactly that: going on for them. It may have blown their world apart. They cannot help it that I have cancer (REFLECTS).

Over there in that wheelbarrow was my life as I knew it. Me - as I knew me. (SHAKING HER HEAD DISMALLY) Gone. Stripped away.

MAN	Your life is still here! I'm still here! I wish I could help you see that.
ONE	I still wake up and in those fuzzy first morning moments, I think it's *before*. Then I reach for my breast, and it's not there (GASPING SOB), and my breath is knocked from me again.
MAN	I still wake up and reach over to you each morning, I find myself thanking every God mentioned in history that you are still by my side.
ONE	Each morning, I swallow down my guttural howl (RELEASES A MOURNING HOWL). Chemotherapy has ravaged my body! A barbaric necessity. I was strong; happy. I was the 'can do' queen. Now I am nothing. Cancer has put all the bits of me that were worthwhile, that contributed to my *living* into a wheelbarrow and taken them away.
MAN	Once this treatment is over, our life will be ours again. We will keep making amazing memories like those over there (GESTURING TO WHEEL-BARROW).
ONE	I am nothing more than a piece of meat that continues to breathe in and out after the butcher has had his way. A slab of meat to be poked and prodded by medical staff for the good of myself. *Myself?* Where did my self go? What about my children? My husband? They deserve more than this old, limp rag of nothing.
MAN	(IN ANGUISH) Oh, my wife! I love you so much. Don't let this struggle consume you.
ONE	He bought a lemon, my man did
	When he fell for the likes of me.

No easy paved road, no honey smooth nights,

No silver lining to be seen.

I got no beauty. Got no left boob.

My womb's dried up and our sex life, too,

My hair--

> ONE GASPS AND COVERS HER
> MOUTH, THEN REGAINS HER
> COMPOSURE AND CONTINUES.

--My hair's all gone, and I cry all day.

The way I howl puts the dogs to shame.

I don't laugh much; rarely offer kind words.

I'm demanding; I'm bossy; I'm sloppy; it's absurd

That he bought a lemon, my man did

When he fell for the likes of me.

Yet, when I say, "I'M A SCRAP OF OLD RAG!"

> ONE STANDS AND SHOUTS THIS
> AT THE WHEELBARROW AND MAN.
> THEN TURNS SLOWLY BACK TO
> THE AUDIENCE AND FINISHES IN
> THE SAME VOICE AS BEFORE.

A scarf of fine silk's all he sees.

> ALLOW A BEAT AND THEN ONE
> EXITS STAGE LEFT. MAN MOVES
> DOWNSTAGE IN FRONT OF THE
> WHEELBARROW.

MAN   (PLEADING WITH AUDIENCE) A scarf of fine silk,

my wife is.

I wish I could help her to see:

That any road travelled,

Any night by her side

Is a silver lining to me!

> MAN LOOKS OFFSTAGE LEFT AND
> DELIVERS THE FOLLOWING TO HIS
> ABSENT WIFE.

A woman of beauty inside and out,

We've shared so much, and there is no doubt,

That while your hair's all gone

And you cry all day,

I just want to steal your pain away.

> MAN TURNS BACK TO AUDIENCE.
> CANCEROUS MASS BEGINS SLOWLY
> CREEPING OVER TO THE WHEEL-
> BARROW BEHIND MAN'S BACK
> AND SHOULD BEGIN TO TRY TO
> COVER IT BY THE LAST LINE.

She makes us laugh, and she rarely complains.

She's courageous; she's inspiring. It's insane

That a scarf of fine silk, my wife is,

Yet she fell for the likes of me.

So, when she says, "I'm a scrap of old rag,"

A scarf of fine silk is all that I see.

WIND RISES IN THE BACKGROUND
AND MAN TURNS TO DISCOVER
WHAT THE CANCEROUS MASS IS
DOING. A BATTLE OVER THE
WHEELBARROW ENSUES BETWEEN
THE CANCEROUS MASS AND MAN.

You can't have her.

PAUSE – STRUGGLE. MAN APPEARS
TO WIN.

(CONVICTED) You can't have her.

PAUSE – STRUGGLE. CANCEROUS
MASS APPEARS TO WIN.

(GETTING ANGRY) You can't have her.

PAUSE – STRUGGLE. MAN APPEARS
TO WIN.

(SHOUTING) You can't have her!

PAUSE – STRUGGLE. MAN APPEARS
TO WIN.

(WORRIED) You can't have her.

PAUSE – STRUGGLE. CANCEROUS
MASS APPEARS TO WIN.

(PLEADING) You can't have her...

PAUSE – STRUGGLE. MAN APPEARS
TO WIN.

(CRYING) You can't have her.

PAUSE – STRUGGLE. CANCEROUS
MASS APPEARS TO WIN.

(YELLING) You can't have her!

A FINAL STRUGGLE. THE BATTLE IS
INTERRUPTED WITHOUT A RESO-
LUTION AS TO WHOM WON THE
BATTLE.

ONE   (OFFSTAGE) Honey?

CANCEROUS MASS AND MAN
FREEZE AT THE SOUND OF
ONE'S VOICE. AFTER A BEAT,
CANCEROUS MASS SINKS TO THE
GROUND AND MAN BRUSHES
HIMSELF OFF, STRAIGHTENS HIS
CLOTHING, SHAKES OFF HIS
EMOTIONS, AND PLASTERS A
SMILE ON HIS FACE.

MAN   (COMPOSED) I will be right there!

LIGHTS FADE OUT AS MAN
CROSSES AND EXITS STAGE LEFT.

SCENE 8

IT IS AFTERNOON. LIGHTS COME
UP ON TWO, THREE AND FOUR
SITTING AT A TABLE IN THE COFFEE
SHOP WITH THEIR RESPECTIVE
BEVERAGES.

WAITER CAN BE CLEANING AND
WIPING DOWN ANOTHER TABLE
DURING THE FOLLOWING.

FOUR   I can't wait to see her.

THREE   Me, too! I saw her the other day when she
                finished her treatment. She's looking quite
                good. I think the new diet I suggested is really
                helping.

TWO   Yes, I was actually quite surprised. But then, I
                was so sure that she was going to die that I
                didn't expect her to look so well. I hope it
                doesn't come back... Do you think it will come
                back?

FOUR   That's just what would happen, knowing my luck.

THREE   Well, she seems fairly positive that it's gone,
                and they say that's half the battle don't they?
                (LOOKING POINTEDLY AT FOUR AND TWO)
                Being positive.

TWO   Yes, but I've found it really hard to be positive
                since Garry left. I can't blame Garry for doing
                it, though. Maybe if I'd worked harder at being
                a better wife and mother--

FOUR   Oh, nonsense! Maybe *he* should have worked
                harder at keeping his dick in his dacks.

THREE GIGGLES, THEN STIFLES IT
QUICKLY.

THREE	I know that it's hard right now, but one day you will realise that you are better off without him. Trust me. You will discover just how much you have to offer someone; the *right* someone.
TWO	I really don't feel like I have anything to offer anybody. Garry was my whole world. Even though I tried to do everything for him, it wasn't enough. I don't even really know how to look after April. He gave me direction and told me what to do. When I am home, I keep sitting on the edge of my chair waiting for his voice to give me my next task. But there's nothing because he's not there. I don't even know who I am anymore. Maybe I should find some way to get him back; being Garry's wife was my whole life.
FOUR	Well, you shouldn't have let that man's happiness become your entire existence, should you?
THREE	Now, it's time for you to build a new life: a new identity.
TWO	But how? I married Garry when I was 18.
FOUR	I wish I could do that.
TWO	(TAKEN ABACK) Do what? Marry Garry?
FOUR	(HORRIFIED) No! I wish I could build a new life: a new identity! Being me is fairly hard you know! If you could see what I have to go through each day--
TWO	Oh, so you *were* listening!
FOUR	(CONDESCENDING) Yes, dear, God gives you two ears and one mouth, so you can listen twice as much as you speak.

TWO AND FOUR FREEZE WHILE

	THREE RUMMAGES THROUGH HER HANDBAG AND SPEAKS.
THREE	(ASIDE) She listens? HA! She thinks her life is so hard? At least she has children. And I'd do a better job raising them if I ever had the chance. I just don't understand why Mark and I don't get to be parents. Now *that's* a struggle that I wouldn't wish upon anyone.
	UNFREEZE. ONE ENTERS WITH BOTH A CALICO AND A SILK SCARF HANGING OUT OF HER HANDBAG. SHE TAKES A SEAT IN THE EMPTY CHAIR.
ONE	Hi, sorry I'm late!
	THE WAITER COMES OVER TO TAKE HER ORDER, BUT SHE WAVES HIM AWAY.
ONE	I can't stay long. Boy, am I glad to see you guys!
TWO	It's good to see you alive and well, too.
THREE	You look fantastic! Is it the carrots? It's the carrots, isn't it?
ONE	Thanks, I feel a bit stronger every day.
FOUR	Where's your man?
ONE	Oh, he'll be along soon enough (GLANCING OVER HER SHOULDER TO SEE IF HE IS ALREADY THERE). He had to run some errands first.
FOUR	So your chemo is done, then?
ONE	Yep! Done and dusted.
THREE	And radiation?

ONE   That too.

FOUR   Thank goodness! I really don't think that I could
                    have taken it had it gone on much longer! I am
                    so glad that whole ordeal is finally over.

ONE   Over? (CONFUSED) I don't know that it will ever
                    be over.

TWO   Oh, my goodness! It's come back, hasn't it? I
                    knew this would happen. Is it terminal?

                              ONE TURNS TO TWO SHOCKED,
                              BUT THEN ONE, TWO, AND THREE
                              FREEZE FRAME.

FOUR   (ASIDE) *Great!* Here we go again. (GESTURE TO
                    TWO) She's going to lose it and go on and on
                    about death and (GESTURE TO THREE) she's
                    going to start ranting about healthy this and
                    healthy that and (LOOKING AT ONE) She's....
                    Well, she's important to me, but I am so sick
                    and tired of every conversation being about
                    her!

                              UNFREEZE

THREE   It hasn't come back, has it? (TO TWO) I'm sure
                    that's not what she meant

ONE   No, (LOOKING AROUND THE TABLE AND
                    SHAKING HER HEAD) that's not what I meant.
                    I guess what I mean is that it will never be over,
                    not for me. (ONE BEGINS TO THINK ABOUT IT
                    AND BECOMES UNCOMFORTABLE AND
                    FATIGUED) Everything is different now. Everything
                    has changed.

TWO   (SYMPATHETICALLY) It's been such a hard time,
                    for you, hasn't it?

ONE	Yeah, it has, but it's been hard for you, too.
	TWO LOOKS AT THE FLOOR EMBARRASSED.
FOUR	(LOUDLY) And for me.
THREE	Yes, we *all* know how hard it's been for *you*.
ONE	(GIGGLES) Oh, I've missed you guys so much. I am so blessed.
FOUR	Yeah, right!
ONE	I'm serious! I am blessed.
TWO	Blessed? I don't think anyone would see what you've gone through as a blessing... you nearly died.
ONE	(REASSURINGLY) But I didn't die. That's why I am blessed. And I have all of you.
FOUR	Well, who wouldn't love 12 months of being looked after?
TWO	(EXASPERATED) Oh, for goodness sake! We all know it wasn't that simple.
	ONCE THE WORDS ARE OUT, TWO CLASPS HER HANDS OVER HER MOUTH IN SHOCK. FOUR SHOCKED.
FOUR	Oh... oh... I don't know...
ONE	You're right. It's not that simple. I feel as if I am looking at life through different eyes now. I *need* to look at life through different eyes now.
THREE	I think that we are all learning to look at life in a new way. I know Mark and I are. We have to...

FOUR	It's about counting your blessings I think.
	MAN ENTERS THE COFFEE SHOP, WALKS OVER TO ONE AND PLACES HIS HAND ON HER SHOULDER. SHE IS CLEARLY DRAINED, BUT SHE LOOKS UP AND SMILES AT HIM.
ONE	Yes! I am showered in blessings (LOOKING AT FOUR) when I take the time to look for them.
	FOUR LOOKS BEHIND HERSELF, TRYING TO WORK OUT WHO ONE IS TALKING TO. REALISES THE DIG IS DIRECTED AT HER AND IS ASTONISHED.
TWO	(TO FOUR) Life sure can change before you realise it. (TO THE OTHERS) I'm thankful that I have all of you for friends as well, especially with what's happened with Garry. You know what? I think I am going to be okay.
THREE	(WARMLY TO TWO) You never know how strong you are until you have to be.
FOUR	(TRYING TO JOIN IN) That is so true, I'm always telling people that. Just the other day--
	TWO, THREE AND FOUR BEGIN MIMING CONVERSATION.
ONE	(ASIDE) None of us choose the burdens we have to carry in life, they just come. But if I did have a choice, would I choose this again? For me, maybe other burdens would be harder to bear? And if I had to trade some of my blessings to avoid this burden, would I? Maybe this burden is what I have to bear in order to have my blessings?

MAN   Thank goodness for your wisdom. Come on honey, we'd better get going.

> ALL OF THE WOMEN STAND TO LEAVE. THEY SAY GOOD-BYE. ONE DROPS THE SCARVES ON THE FLOOR. MAN REACHES TO PICK THEM UP. THREE AND FOUR EXIT TALKING TO EACH OTHER. TWO STARES AT THE SCARVES.

TWO   I bet you're glad that you can get rid of those scarves, now.

> ONE SMILES AND LOOKS AT MAN. TWO EXITS.

ONE   These? Oh, no. I will be keeping these a while longer. Yes. I think I will.

> ONE LOOKS DOWN AT THE FINE SILK SCARF AND THE TATTY CALICO SCARF/RAG. MAN PUTS HIS ARM AROUND HER, AND THEY STAND STILL ON THE STAGE LOOKING AT THE SCARVES.

> *BLACK-OUT*

> "TOGETHER SONG" BEGINS TO PLAY.

> *CURTAIN*

About the Author

On December 15, 2011, at age 34, Briohne Sykes was diagnosed with Stage III Mucinal and Ductal Carcinoma. She then survived a Mastectomy with Aux Clearance (25 lymph nodes removed), Chemotherapy (FEC-D), Radiation (25 sessions), Hysterectomy including Oophorectomy, Lymphoedeama Management, Depression, and Anxiety.

Now on the recovery side of treatment, Briohne spends her time enjoying the sweet life of living past your used by date, writing as much as she can, and passionately embracing all the delicious bits of each day.

Moving forward, Briohne is hoping that her play *Powerfully Fragile* will have some community impact, that her health will remain stable and that she will continue making amazing memories "like those over there".

"Writing Powerfully Fragile was a beautiful experience for me. I made a very close friend through my diagnosis, who I recently lost to the same disease. In reflecting on the poems and camaraderie we shared, I wanted to create a performance piece that would emanate that feeling to other cancer patients. Moving forward, I wanted to highlight community viewpoints to encourage the audience to reflect not only upon their attitudes about cancer, but also all life's burdens. I want every person who participates in this play to feel that they know one of the women on stage."

- Briohne Sykes, Playwright

www.ingramcontent.com/pod-product-compliance
Lightning Source LLC
Chambersburg PA
CBHW021445090426
42739CB00009B/1659

* 9 7 8 0 9 8 7 5 8 7 7 0 1 *